We Can Do
Mitzvos
from
Aleph
to
Tav

by Yael Zoldan
illustrated by Shira Allen

FELDHEIM
JERUSALEM · NEW YORK

א ב ג ד ה ו ז ח ט י כ ל מ נ ס ע פ צ ק ר ש ת

*This book is dedicated
with love to my children.
May you grow to be righteous,
kind and happy with your lot.*

*And to my husband, Mark,
who is all that already,
and even more to me.*

ISBN 978-1-59826-395-4

Copyright © 2009 by Yael Zoldan

FELDHEIM PUBLISHERS
POB 43163
Jerusalem, Israel

208 Airport Executive Park
Nanuet, NY 10954

www.feldheim.com

10 9 8 7 6 5 4 3 2 1

Let's take a look at the Aleph Beis,
Let's read it letter by letter,
We'll learn a mitzvah for each אוֹת,
So we can be better and better!

Aleph is for Achdus,
Together as one we stick,

אַחְדוּת

Beis is for Bikur Cholim,
That's visiting the sick!

בִּקּוּר חוֹלִים

ג

Gimmel's Gemilus Chesed,
Being kind and good,

גְּמִילוּת חֶסֶד

ד

Dalet is for Derech Eretz,
Acting the way we should.

דֶּרֶךְ אֶרֶץ

ה

Hei — Hachnasas Orchim,
Welcoming a guest,

הַכְנָסַת אוֹרְחִים

וֹ

Vav is V'ahavta,
Loving each other best.

וְאָהַבְתָּ

Zayin is for Zerizus,
To do a Mitzvah — run!

זְרִיזוּת

Ches is the אוֹת for Chanukah —
Menorahs, Latkes... FUN!

חֲנֻכָּה

Tes is for the Tallis
Abba wears in shul each day,

טַלִּית

Yud is for Yir'as Hashem,
Serve Hashem in every way.

יִרְאַת ה'

כ

Kaf's for keeping Kosher,
The only food we eat,

כָּשֵׁר

ל

Lamed — Limud Torah,
Learning Torah is so sweet!

לִמּוּד תּוֹרָה

Mem is for Megillah,
Which we read on Purim day,

מְגִלָּה

נ

Nun is for Nikayon,
Clean and neat we stay.

נִקָּיוֹן

Samech is for Sukkos,
When we eat outside all week,

סֻכּוֹת

Ayin is for Anavah,
Be humble and be meek.

עֲנָוָה

Peh's the אֹות for Pesach,
With Matzos and Maror and more,

פֶּסַח

Tzaddi's for Tzedakah,
That's helping out the poor.

צְדָקָה

ק

Kuf is for Keriyas Shema,
We say in bed each night,

קְרִיאַת שְׁמַע

ר

Reish is for Rodef Shalom,
That's trying not to fight!

רוֹדֵף שָׁלוֹם

Shin's the אוֹת for Shabbos,
Our favorite day of the week,

שַׁבָּת

And Tav is for Tefillah,
To Hashem Himself we speak!

תְּפִלָּה

Now we've read from Aleph to Tav,
There's so much we can do!
We learned a mitzvah for each אוֹת,
To be a top-notch Jew!